THE BIG BOOK OF STOCK TRADING STRATEGIES

MATTHEW R. KRATTER

WWW.TRADER.UNIVERSITY

For my children

CONTENTS

DISCLAIMER

Neither Little Cash Machines LLC, nor any of its directors, officers, shareholders, personnel, representatives, agents, or independent contractors (collectively, the "Operator Parties") are licensed financial advisers, registered investment advisers, or registered broker-dealers. None of the Operator Parties are providing investment, financial, legal, or tax advice, and nothing in this book or at www.Trader.University (henceforth, "the Site") should be construed as such by you. This book and the Site should be used as educational tools only and are not replacements for professional investment advice. The full disclaimer can be found at the end of this book.

YOUR FREE GIFT

Thanks for purchasing my book!

As a way of showing my appreciation, I want to send you a FREE BONUS CHAPTER that contains everything that you need to start using my stock trading strategies.

In this free bonus chapter, you will learn:

- How to use online screeners to find the best stocks to trade
- How to set up a trading chart using free online resources
- Tricks to make the trading strategies even more profitable
- A free video tutorial on the Day Sniper day trading strategy
- And much, much more

Enter your email at the link below and I will send you a free copy of this Bonus Chapter:

http://www.trader.university/big-book/

ONE

THE BEST WAY TO LEARN HOW TO TRADE STOCKS

What's the best way to learn how to trade stocks?

It's quite simple, actually.

Pick one specific trading strategy, and focus all of your time and attention on it, until you have mastered it.

Then, and only then, try out another trading strategy.

Too often, new traders jump from one strategy to another, never staying in one place long enough to learn from their mistakes, as well as from their winning trades.

In this book, I have collected the most popular trading strategies from my previous books:

- The Rubber Band Stocks Strategy
- The Rocket Stocks Strategy
- The Day Sniper Trading Strategy

If you slowly work your way through this book, and put into practice what you are learning, you will emerge on the other side as a much more mature and confident trader.

As you work your way through the book, feel free to email me at matt@trader.university with your questions and comments.

I've trained thousands of new traders over the years, and I'm here to help you too.

All of the trading strategies in this book are easy to learn, simple to follow, and will teach you the discipline that is essential to becoming a successful trader.

A final note before we get started:

When you are first learning how to trade, it is important not to focus on the money.

You should focus on only 3 things:

- Your entry price
- Your profit target
- Your stop loss

If you can focus on just these 3 things, then the money will begin to take care of itself.

It's now time to get started with our first trading strategy.

TWO

RUBBER BAND STOCKS (HOW TO TRADE BOUNCING STOCKS)

When Warren Buffett tells us that we need to be "greedy when others are fearful," he is really just saying that we need to buy stocks when others are selling stocks.

This sounds easy in principle, but how exactly do you do it in real life?

The Rubber Band Stocks Strategy is one answer to this question.

When trading this strategy, I use Bollinger Bands, which look like this:

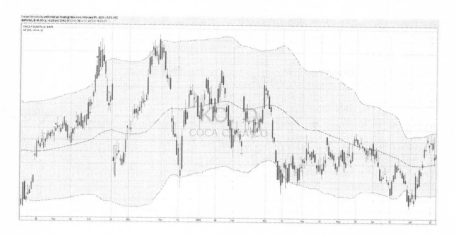

You don't need to know exactly how Bollinger Bands are calculated for now.

All you need to know is that when a stock closes below the lower Bollinger Band, it should always get your attention. Here is a stock closing two different times below the lower Bollinger Band:

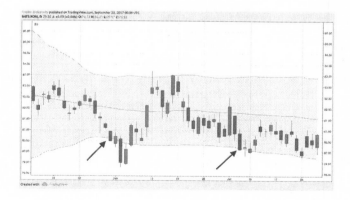

Each bar or "candlestick" represents one trading day. If the candle-stick is red, it means that the stock's closing price is lower than its opening price. If the candlestick is green, it means that the stock's closing price is higher than its opening price. The top of the "wick" shows the stock's daily high price, and the bottom of the "wick" shows the stock's daily low price.

I've put a big arrow on the chart above to show you the day that the stock closed below the lower Bollinger Band. The bottom of the red part of the candlestick is the closing price.

You can use paid sources like http://www.tradestation.com for Bollinger Band charts, but you can also use free sources like http://www.freestockcharts.com. Just be sure to use daily bars, and to set your Bollinger Band to use an 80-period look-back and plus/minus 2 standard deviations for the band width.

Feel free to email me at matt@trader.university if you need help with this set-up.

As I said before, when a stock closes below the lower Bollinger Band, it should always get your attention. A close below the lower band means one of two things:

1. The stock is ready to snap back up like a stretched rubber band; or
2. The stock is ready to trend downwards.

In order to get a stock to trade below the lower Bollinger Band, it takes an unusual amount of selling pressure. Sometimes that selling pressure is justified, such as those cases where the stock is rapidly going to zero (think Enron or Lehman).

And sometime that selling pressure IS NOT justified (for example, traders get spooked by reports of pink slime in McDonald's hamburgers, but McDonald's apologizes, moves on, and continues to print money).

A close below the lower Bollinger Band is always a signal that we need to do further research on the stock in order to see if everyone has temporarily thrown in the towel or "capitulated."

"Capitulation" is what happens when a trader has lost so much money on a trade and is in so much psychic pain, that he hits the sell button.

Fear, disgust, panic.

Those are the kinds of emotions that get a stock to trade below its lower Bollinger Band. Then there are those sellers that are being forced to sell by their brokers, due to margin calls.

Why do we want to see capitulation in a stock?

Simple- – that is what happens right before a stock bounces. When the last seller has sold, the stock is extremely stretched like a rubber band.

It is ready to snap back.

So how do you buy when everyone is selling?

Simple: you know that everyone is selling when a stock closes below the lower Bollinger Band.

Should you always buy a stock that has just closed below the lower Bollinger Band?

Absolutely not.

We need to focus only on those stocks that have the highest probability of snapping back.

∼

So how do you separate the fake rubber band stocks from the real ones?

Here's how:

Let's take a stock XYZ that has just had a daily close below the lower Bollinger Band, as we discussed in the last section. There has obviously been a lot of selling pressure to get the stock below the lower band.

But have traders thrown in the towel or "capitulated"? If not, the stock might continue lower as they finally DO throw in the towel and sell their positions.

Only stocks where traders have already thrown in the towel have the best chance of rallying.

What I'm looking for is stocks that have closed below the lower Bollinger Band, where trader sentiment is also bearish.

In order to figure out how bearish traders are on a stock, I use the following websites:

http://www.stocktwits.com/

http://finance.yahoo.com/mb/

Go to each of these websites, type in the stock ticker, and start to get a feel for what other traders are thinking about the stock.

Traders should be saying things like:

- "She's going down."
- "This stock is acting scary. Be careful out there."
- "I'm out, live to fight another day."
- "I'm staying on the sidelines, too risky to enter here."

Do NOT buy the stock if lots of traders are saying things like:

- "Adding more here, expecting a bounce soon."
- "This is an easy double in 6 months."
- "Just one announcement about a strategic partner will send this one rocketing higher."
- "This sell-off is way overdone."
- "Starting a position. Really like it at these prices."

If a stock is trading below the lower Bollinger Band, and the majority of traders are bearish on the stock, then you have the perfect set-up for a stock that has a high probability of snapping back.

Now that you have found a stock that has closed below the lower Bollinger Band and that has bearish trader sentiment, you are ready to trade.

I usually do my research the night before, and then come up with a list of stocks to buy when the market opens in the morning.

Often I will enter limit orders (e.g. "Buy MSFT at 40.00 limit") the night before and then go to sleep.

That way, there is no need to get up early if I don't feel like it. If the stock trades at my price, my trade will be executed. If not, there's always another trade around the corner.

Decide how much of your trading account you want to put into each stock signal. 1% or 2% is considered pretty conservative.

Anything over 10% is pretty aggressive.

You need to know your own financial situation, your own comfort level, and consult with your own financial advisor.

To make the math easy, let's say that your trading account has $20,000 in it.

You feel like trading aggressively, so you decide to put 10% of your account (or $2,000) into buying Microsoft at 40. So you put in a limit order to buy $2000 divided by $40/share, or 50 shares.

Put in your limit order to buy the stock at the same price that it closed at below the lower Bollinger Band.

Now let me explain how I manage a trade once it is on.

After entering below the lower Bollinger Band, I almost always wait for a daily close above the middle Bollinger Band to exit. Most of the time, this is at a profit, like here:

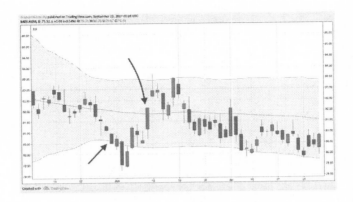

Though sometimes it is also at a loss, like here:

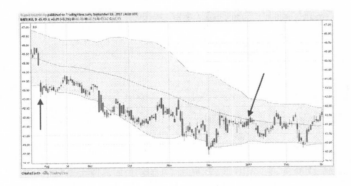

Again if you want to sleep in (especially if you live on the West Coast, and don't want to wake up at 6:30 am for the market open), take a look at where the middle band is the night before. If it's at 45, then enter your sell limit order for 45.01, and feel free to sleep in.

Or you can do what I do. I wait for the stock to close above the middle band.

Then, before I go to bed that night, I enter a sell limit order at that closing price. It may take a day or two to get executed, but at least I am not glued to my screen.

Never exiting before the stock closes above the middle band is the most aggressive way of trading. That's how I often do it because I believe that it maximizes profits over the long term.

But most traders will also want to include a stop loss, i.e. a price at which to exit a losing trade before it gets too bad.

There are different ways to pick your stop loss price level. For example, if you are losing money on a trade, you can exit if the stock trades down 2% from your entry price. Or 5%, or even 10%.

A lot of this will depend on how much of your trading account you have put into a single stock trade.

If you only have 2% of your trading account in a trade, a loss of 10% on the trade will only be a loss of 0.20% for the trading account as a whole.

On the other hand, if you have 50% of your trading account in a trade, a loss of 10% on the trade will be a loss of 5% for the trading account.

Instead of using a percentage stop, you can also use Bollinger Bands to set your stop.

Normally, Bollinger Bands are set +2 and − 2 standard deviations below the middle band. But you can also add in some bands at +3 and − 3 standard deviations (the blue bands below):

Or you can add in bands at +4 and − 4 standard deviations (purple below):

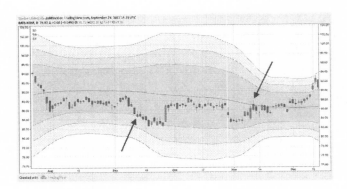

If you want to use the lower – 3 Bollinger Band as your stop, when you enter a trade, write down where the lower – 3 Bollinger Band is trading **on that day**. You can then use that as your stop. If the stock trades below that price level, then you exit immediately. Or if you want to be more aggressive, wait until the stock does a daily close below the – 3 Bollinger Band, which will of course be moving around.

If you want to be even more aggressive, you can apply the same method to the – 4 Bollinger Band.

If you make the lower band wide enough, you'll be pretty much trading like me- – most of the time, I wait for a close above the middle band to exit a trade, whether it is a winning trade or a losing trade.

An alternate stop loss method is to use a time stop. If, after you enter a stock, it does not rally back up to the middle band after 10-15 trading days (you can experiment with the exact number), exit the position immediately at a profit or loss.

The advantage of a time stop is that your capital will never be tied up for too long in a stock that is going nowhere.

You can also try combining a time stop loss with a price stop loss. For example, you exit your position after 10 days (time stop loss), or the moment it loses 5% from your entry (price stop loss)-- whichever comes first.

A final note: in a true bear market, many stocks will pierce their lower Bollinger Band and then keep selling off, sometimes even for many months. If you want to be conservative, do not trade the Rubber Band Stocks Strategy in a bear market.

If you want to be aggressive in a bear market, you can short stocks that close below their lower Bollinger Bands, rather than buying them (even if trader sentiment is bearish).

Set your stop loss at the middle band at entry, or use the middle band as a trailing stop. If the stock closes above the middle band, you will cover (exit) your short position.

How do you know if you are in a bear market?

There are 2 easy methods that will give you an indication.

The first is this: if you have 3 losing trades in a row using the Rubber Band Stocks Strategy, take 30 days off, as you may be in a bear market. After 30 days have passed, you can try again (preferably trading smaller size).

The second method for identifying a bear market is to look at this chart and type in the symbol SPY:

https://www.tradingview.com/chart/7PeD7Qrd/

If the blue line (50 day moving average of SPY) is below the red line (200 day moving average of SPY), you are in a bear market, and should be cautious.

If the blue line is above the red line, you are probably in a bull market, and can use the Rubber Band Stock Strategy with confidence (always trade with a stop loss, of course, unless you are an advanced trader).

All of this sounds a lot more complicated on paper than it actually is in practice.

If you want to see how this works in real life, try paper trading in a virtual stock trading account or try an experimental trade using just 1% or less of your trading account.

Now let's take a look at a few real trading examples that took place in late 2015.

On October 26, 2015, PANW closed below the lower Bollinger Band, as you can see here:

https://www.tradingview.com/chart/U3rZnAa3/

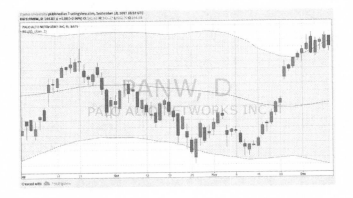

At the time, however, sentiment was still too bullish on the stock to make it a buy.

By November 10-13, trader sentiment was finally turning negative as you can see here, in tweets taken from www.stocktwits.com/symbol/PANW:

- November 10, 7:41 am $PANW Next stop 140's.
  Bearish.
- November 10, 2:35 pm $PANW is this company doomed? Everyone talking it down CNBC bearish. What would be a catalyst driving this higher?
- November 11, 7:22 am The 3-month chart for $PANW looks like absolute death. Absolutely no positive catalysts in site (other than ER) and no momentum at all.
- November 12, 10:05 am $PANW setting up for a brilliant short. Bearish
- November 12, 10:32 am Looking at the trends would not buy this one. It's expected to slump 10-20% post earnings. Bearish
- November 12, 11:44 am $PANW will be the next

darling of the talking heads to crash and burn. All the hot stocks at crazy multiples get hammered after ER's lately.

- November 12, 1:26 pm Don't go down with the ship. Bearish
- November 13, 7:47 am bought Nov 27 $141 put for 2.50. Bearish

Bearish sentiment like this stretched PANW downwards like a rubber band.

While these traders were bearish on PANW (and thus presumably selling their stock), you could have been loading up on it.

On November 13 (at the peak of trader bearish sentiment), PANW closed at 156.64. You could have bought it at the close, and sold it just a few days later on November 23, when it closed above the middle Bollinger Band at 172.02.

Here's another example: on October 27, 2015, CPLA closed below the lower Bollinger Band.

On the same day, trader sentiment was also quite negative as you can see here, in tweets taken from http://www.stocktwits.com/symbol/CPLA:

- October 27, 7:40 am Still has great downside potential. Stock not worth more than $40 IMO. Especially when you have major holder dumping $15 million $CPLA Bearish.

- October 28, 11:54 am Lots of stocks rebounding + moving higher last few weeks, but for-profit education not among them $CPLA $LRN $APOL

On October 28, CPLA closed at 44.22. You could have bought it at the close (or at an even lower price the very next day), and sold it on December 10, when it closed above the middle Bollinger Band at 50.24.

YUM is another great example. On August 11, 2015, YUM closed below the lower Bollinger Band.

At the time, however, trader sentiment was still too bullish on the stock to make it a buy.

By early October 2015, trader sentiment had sharply deteriorated, as you can see here in tweets taken from www.stocktwits.com/symbol/YUM:

- October 7, 6:08 am $YUM this stock should be worth 50$ on a generous multiple. Worth 30$ for sum of parts. Sell this into oblivion. Bearish.
- October 7, 6:26 am $YUM Sell it guys. It's not good. Bearish
- October 7, 6:35 am $YUM This is dangerous. Forget it. Bearish
- October 7, 6:46 am $YUM Who is right mind would buy? 3 day rule? Bearish.

- October 7, 6:56 am $YUM There is no bottom right now. Bearish.
- October 8, 12:30 pm $YUM too disgusting out the sellers too strong too heavy.

On October 8, YUM closed at 67.46. You could have bought it at the close, and sold it on December 4, when it finally closed above the middle Bollinger Band at 76.14.

Our final example is TMUS, which closed below the lower Bollinger Band on November 10, 2015.

At the time, however, sentiment was still too bullish on the stock to make it a buy.

By December 4, trader sentiment had finally turned negative enough, as you can see here, in tweets taken from http://www.stocktwits.com/symbol/TMUS:

- December 2, 6:34 am $TMUS Setting up for the next leg down.
- December 3, 8:49 am $TMUS That's all the loss I can stand. This stock will boom once this company is sold... Until then I'm out. Bearish.
- December 4, 3:55 pm $TMUS Gravity is in charge? Bearish.

On December 4, TMUS closed at 35.45. You could have bought it at the close, and sold it on December 17, when it finally closed above the middle Bollinger Band at 39.20.

~

You are now ready to trade Rubber Band Stocks Strategy yourself. All you need to do is to find stocks that meet the following requirements:

1. The stock has just closed below the lower Bollinger Band (make sure that your Bollinger Band indicator is formatted so that it is using an 80 day moving average, and each band is 2 standard deviations out). A good free resource is http://www.FreeStockCharts.com.
2. Look for extreme bearish trader sentiment surrounding your stock at http://www.stocktwits.com and http://finance.yahoo.com/mb/.

That's it!

Make sure that you review this chapter before putting on your first trade.

Also before you start, make sure that you know how to size your trade, and how to manage your trade using a profit target and a stop loss.

If you do not have a lot of trading experience, I suggest that you first practice trading the Rubber Band Stocks Strategy without using real money.

Any number of brokers will let you open up a practice (paper-trading) account.

I have not tried them myself, but my students have reported good things about the paper trading accounts available here:

https://www.thinkorswim.com/t/pm-registration.html

THREE

ROCKET STOCKS (THE SHORTEST PATH TO WEALTH IN THE STOCK MARKET)

A "rocket stock" is a stock that goes straight up over a short period of time.

Following a rocket stock is like watching a force of nature-- a volcanic eruption, or a supernova filling the sky.

On the way up, a rocket stock makes everyone rub their eyes in disbelief.

Remember Tesla in April 2013? It went from 44 to 164 in just six months.

Or YELP in June 2013? It went from 27 to 75 in just five months.

Rocket stocks are the shortest path to wealth in the stock market.

Yet many traders and investors miss out on them.

Why?

Because there is nothing more difficult than buying a high P/E stock that keeps hitting new all-time highs.

Our psychology holds us back. Our common sense holds us back.

And the talking heads on TV certainly don't help. They keep telling us to avoid Amazon because it has a P/E of 300. Or to avoid Tesla because it is losing so much money that it doesn't even have a P/E.

If you are Warren Buffett investing in a mature company, the P/E matters. If you are holding a rocket stock for a few weeks or months, nothing matters less than the P/E.

In fact, a rocket stock usually looks expensive all the way up. As a result, newbie traders keep waiting for a "pullback" to enter.

But when that pullback finally comes, it is usually suicidal to take it.

BBRY (the company that made the Blackberry) went from 5 to 150 in five years. That's the kind of move that can turn $10,000 into $300,000.

But then it went down 95% over the next four years.

If you bought on a pullback, you were wiped out. If you waited to buy until its P/E was reasonable, you were wiped out.

All the way up, there were doubters and skeptics.

All the way down, there were true believers (who kept doubling down on their losing positions). All the way down, stock analysts and investment newsletters kept proclaiming how cheap the stock was.

A stock can get really cheap on its way to zero.

As you will learn in this chapter, a cheap rocket stock is a trap. You will be left holding the bag, while Wall Street moves on to the next growth story.

Rocket stocks are counter-intuitive. They don't follow the normal rules that you learn on CNBC.

If you don't know how to trade them properly, they will wipe you out.

But if you know the secrets, rocket stocks can make you extremely rich.

In this chapter, I am going to share all of those secrets. I am going to tell you exactly how I have been trading rocket stocks for the last 20 years.

And because I don't want you to be the sucker that Wall Street leaves holding the bag, I am also going to teach you when to get out.

When to enter, when to take profits, and when to just get out.

As you will see, it is actually quite simple.

You don't need to be a stock analyst, or an expert in some new technology.

You simply need to learn how to listen to the market.

All stocks that go up a lot have one thing in common.

It is not that they are all tech stocks, or commodity stocks, or Chinese stocks, or whatever.

All stocks that go up a lot keep hitting new 52 week highs, or even new all-time highs, along the way. This is an obvious fact.

Yet have you ever bought a stock that was trading at a new all-time high?

It's not easy. 95% of traders are psychologically unable to do it.

Yet there is something wonderful and magical about a stock at all-time new highs.

It is like a rocket escaping from the Earth's gravitational field: the higher it goes, the less there is to hold it back.

At a new high, everyone who owns the stock has a profit.

All of the losers are gone: they have already exited at a loss, or at their breakeven price.

At new highs, there are only happy traders and investors left.

Well, except for one group of traders that no one pities too much: the short-sellers.

At a new all-time high, everyone who has shorted the stock previously now has a losing trade on their hands. They are sweating every tick as the stock moves higher.

And at a certain price, they will be forced to "cover" their shorts, by buying back the shares that they had previously sold short.

Such buying only adds more fuel to the fire, driving the stock even higher, and forcing out more short sellers.

Meanwhile, a stock that has recently moved up a lot begins to be featured on CNBC and discussed by online commentators. This publicity brings in a new wave of buyers, which continues to drive the stock higher and make it hit new 52 week or all-time highs.

Eventually, the "fear of missing out" (FOMO) takes over. At this point, panicked buying can make the stock shoot up almost vertically.

Like a rocket.

Next we will learn how to find these rocket stocks just before they are ready to really blast off.

~

In the previous section, we discussed our first stock selection filter for finding rocket stocks:

Only consider stocks that are hitting new 52-week highs, or new all-time highs.

If you're having trouble finding a list of these stocks, shoot me an email at matt@trader.university, and I can send you the most current list.

Now it is time to add another filter:

Look for a surge in volume that confirms the break-out.

The best potential rocket stocks will experience a surge in volume as they begin to break out to new highs. Look for daily volume that is anywhere from 4x to 40x average daily volume, especially on the break-out day.

Most charting programs will allow you to easily calculate and chart average daily volume for a stock. I like to use a look-back period of 60 days when calculating daily average volume.

When Tesla broke out to new highs on April 1, 2013, it traded 14,105,873 shares. That was more than 7x its 60-day trailing average daily volume of 1,921,674.

When YELP broke out to new highs on May 2, 2013, it traded 10,145,781 shares, which was more than 8x its 60-day trailing average daily volume of 1,242,988.

When a rocket stock is hitting new highs on higher than average volume, it will often gap up at the beginning of its move. This is not absolutely necessary, but it is often a sign of huge pent-up demand for the stock.

In the following chart, you can see YELP gapping up on 2 separate days, each with above-average volume:

Daily volume is shown by the vertical bars at the bottom of the chart. 60-day average volume is shown by the shaded blue area at the bottom of the chart.

In the following chart, you can see Tesla gapping up on a huge spike in volume:

Prior to April 1, 2013, Tesla had never closed above 40.00. Rather, as you can see in the above chart, 40.00 had always been a "ceiling" or area of upside resistance for the stock.

On April 1, 2013, everything changed. The stock gapped above 40.00 (new all-time highs) on high volume. At that point, 40.00 became the new floor (area of support) for the stock.

Tesla never looked back: it had become a rocket stock. Just a few months later, it would hit 194.00.

When a stock gaps to new highs on higher than average volume, it should always get your attention.

In the next section, we will learn even more filters that you can apply to find the best rocket stocks.

When Tesla gapped to new highs on high volume on April 1, 2013, it had something else going in its favor: it was already in an uptrend.

You've probably heard the expression: "the trend is your friend."

Nowhere is this more true than with a rocket stock.

Sometimes a stock will break out to new 52-week highs, and then immediately head back down, like a crashing rocket.

One way to avoid these false break-outs is to be sure that the break-out has been confirmed by heavier than normal volume, as we discussed in the previous section.

Another way to avoid these false break-outs is to make sure that the stock is in an uptrend.

We know that a stock is in an uptrend if both of the following statements are true:

- **The stock is trading above its 50-day moving average.**
- **The stock's 50-day moving average is above its 200-day moving average.**

To calculate the 50-day moving average, you add up a stock's daily closing price for each of the last 50 trading days (i.e. don't count weekends), and divide by 50:

(price 50 days ago + price 49 days ago + price 48 days + . . . + price yesterday + closing price today) divided by 50.

To calculate the 200-day moving average, you do the same thing: add up the stock's closing price for each of the last 200 trading days, and divide by 200.

Fortunately, you do not need to do this by hand. There are free websites that will do these calculations and then chart them for you.

I especially like www.FreeStockCharts.com and www.TradingView.com.

Feel free to email me at matt@trader.university, if you need any help setting up these charts.

We've already discussed that wonderful day on April 1, 2013 when Tesla gapped up to new highs on high volume. What we can see now is that it was already in an uptrend at the time, which made the trade even more likely to be a winner:

An online version of this image is available here:

www.tradingview.com/x/R64pUIF9/

You can see that on the day of the gap to new highs with high volume, Tesla is trading above its 50-day moving average, and that the 50-day moving average (the blue line) is above its 200-day moving average (the red line).

It is also extremely helpful (though not always necessary) for the stock market to also be in an uptrend at the time, as was the S&P 500 in 2013:

An online version of this image is available here:

www.tradingview.com/x/N8KzGWHi/

You can see that at the same time that Tesla gapped up, the S&P 500 (you can use the ticker of its ETF, which is SPY) was trading above its 50-day moving average; and its 50-day moving average was above its 200-day moving average.

If both a stock and the general markets are in an uptrend (as measured by SPY or QQQ), the trading environment is extremely friendly to rocket stocks. This is a good time to increase your position size and trade more aggressively.

In the next section, we will learn a few more filters to apply to rocket stocks.

We will now discuss how to use market cap and float to find profitable rocket stocks.

Just before it gapped up in April 2013, Tesla had a few other positive things going for it.

It had a relatively small market cap—just over $4 billion at the time.

To put this in perspective, Tesla's current market cap is $32 billion, and Apple's current market cap is over $500 billion.

It is much easier for a stock with a market cap of $4 billion to go up 8x (as Tesla did), than it is for a stock with a $40 billion market cap to go up 8x.

This leads us to our next rule:

Try to find rocket stocks with a market cap of $4 billion or less.

Many large mutual funds and hedge funds cannot even look at a stock if its market cap is less than $5 billion.

However, once a stock reaches $5-10 billion, a whole new set of buyers will come in, driving the stock even higher.

The smaller the market cap, the easier it is for large amounts of money to move the stock.

Our next rule is related to this concept:

Try to find rocket stocks with a small float (where the float is 20% or less of the total shares outstanding).

The "float" is simply the number of shares of a stock that are actually available for trading.

To calculate it, you just take the number of shares outstanding, and subtract closely held shares (which are held by the founders, original investors, and employees).

For example, Tesla's float is currently 104.70 million shares (72%), out of total of 145.88 million total shares outstanding. This means that 41.18 million shares (or 28%) are essentially locked away and do not trade on a daily basis.

You can use this link to look up the float for any stock:

http://finance.yahoo.com/q/ks?s=TSLA+Key+Statistics

Where it says "Get Key Statistics," just enter a new ticker and press "Go." The float and total shares outstanding are listed somewhere in the middle of the far right column.

All things being equal, you want to look for stocks with a float that is less than 20% of its total shares outstanding. This will not be possible for every trade, but it can definitely help you to find short-term winners.

Recent IPO's (stocks that have just started trading on the public markets) will often have floats that are just 10-20% of their shares outstanding.

For example, when Twitter went public, it IPO-ed with just 70 million shares (11.38%) out of total of 615 million shares outstanding.

When the float is this small, it doesn't take much buying to have a huge effect: Twitter went from 45 to 74 in its first 6 weeks of trading.

After an IPO, insiders are usually prohibited from selling their stock for 6-12 months (depending on the company). This provides the perfect window in which to buy a newly IPO-ed rocket stock, watch it soar, and sell it, before the waves of insider selling hit the market.

Always wait for an IPO to start hitting new highs before you buy it. Buying an IPO on a dip is a fool's errand, and will often lead to big losses.

For example, on its first day of trading, Twitter closed at 44.90. It proceeded to sell off for 2 weeks on initial profit taking.

On December 10, 2013, Twitter finally closed at a new all-time trading high (51.99). At this point, every holder of the stock had a profit. Just a few weeks later on December 26, Twitter closed at 73.31.

That is a true rocket stock, and was only made possible by Twitter's very small float.

For recent IPO's, there will not be enough trading history to generate a 50-day or 200-day moving average, so you will not be able to use the "uptrend" criteria that we discussed above.

A small float will allow a stock to shoot up more quickly, but also to crash more quickly. For this reason, it is very important to trade using a stop loss, especially if you are trading a recent IPO.

Buy the IPO when it closes at new all-time highs. You can set yourself an initial stop loss of 5% (i.e. you will exit the trade if the stock sells off more than 5% from your entry price).

From that point on, use a trailing stop. Whenever the stock closes at a new high, calculate a price that is 10% below that, and use that price as your new stop loss. As the stock moves up, your stop loss level will move up too—hence the name "trailing stop."

You can also use a 10-day exponential moving average as a stop loss. Exit your IPO trade on a daily close below this exponential moving average.

I like to use a 10-day exponential moving average here, rather than a regular moving average, as the former will weight recent data more heavily, which will make for a tighter stop.

To summarize: if at all possible, looks for stocks that have a small market cap (less than $4 billion), or a small float (less than 20% of total shares). Even a small increase in incremental demand has the potential to move these stocks up a lot.

~

It is now time to discuss how to use sentiment and short interest to find even more profitable rocket stocks.

In December 2012, Southwest Airlines (LUV) started hitting new highs.

The stock was clearly in an uptrend: it was trading above its 50-day moving average, and its 50-day moving average was above its 200-day moving average.

At the time, I saw this signal, but couldn't stop thinking about Warren Buffett's famous quote:

> "If a capitalist had been present at Kitty Hawk back in the early 1900s, he should have shot Orville Wright. He would have saved his progeny money. But seriously, the airline business has been extraordinary. It has eaten up capital over the past century like almost no other business because people seem to keep coming back to it and putting fresh money in. You've got huge fixed costs, you've got strong labor unions and you've got commodity pricing. That is not a great recipe for success. I have an 800 (free call) number now that I call if I get the urge to buy an airline stock. I call at two in the morning and I say: 'My name is Warren and I'm an aeroholic.' And then they talk me down."

> www.forbes.com/sites/tedreed/2013/05/13/buffett-decries-airline-investing-even-though-at-worst-he-broke-even

Buffett was obviously talking about investing in airlines (rather than holding them for a trade). Nevertheless, when I was thinking of buying some LUV, I felt like I should first call an "aeroholic" hot line like Buffett.

A few months after LUV first broke to new highs, a few other airlines began to break out to the upside as well, including United Airlines (UAL), Spirit Airlines (SAVE), and American Airlines (AAL). If a whole industry starts to hit new 52-week highs on increased volume, you really have to pay attention.

Unfortunately I missed the trade: I could not bring myself to buy an airlines stock.

It was a good lesson for me to learn:

The trades that I hate the most often turn out to be the biggest winners.

If you think about it, this makes perfect sense. I am an experienced trader and investor, and so if I hate a trade, I probably have a very good reason for doing so.

And other smart people in the markets are probably avoiding the trade for the same or similar reasons. In this case, I even had Warren Buffett himself on my side.

When a stock is widely hated, no one owns it. Everyone who used to hold the stock, and now agrees with us, has already sold the stock. In most cases, this will mean that most market participants (even closet indexers) are underweight the name.

As a result, there is only one direction that the stock can go, and that is up.

I felt the same way about Home Depot (HD) and Lowes (LOW) in early 2012.

Both were hitting new highs on high volume, but I still hated them.

At the time, housing was still in the doldrums in the wake of the 2008-2009 financial crisis. Short sales were happening all around the country, and even those who were able to hold on to their homes probably didn't have the extra cash needed for home improvement.

We now know that late 2011 was the bottom in housing for most markets. It has been straight up since then, and the stocks of Home Depot and Lowes have benefited.

The market is a forward-looking machine. It always begins to price in good news months before that good news shows up in the economic reports and on CNBC.

If you wait for the good news to hit the front pages, you will have missed the bulk of the trade.

That is why 52-week highs and new all-time highs are such a powerful tool. They allow you to read the footprints of what the really smart money is doing.

If a stock is hitting new all-time highs, there is usually a very good reason for it.

If you wait for that good reason to become widely acknowledged, you will have missed the trade.

So the next time you are looking at a stock that is hitting new 52-week highs on high volume, flip on CNBC and see what they are saying about it. Is your stock in a widely hated or ridiculed industry? That's a good sign.

Or tell your friends that you are thinking of making the trade. If everyone laughs at you or shakes their heads in disbelief at your stupidity, you probably have a very good trade on your hands.

Do you yourself hate the trade? Do you feel slightly sick to your stomach at the thought of buying the stock? If so, that could be one of the best signs that the trade is going to be a big winner.

Stocks that are widely hated are also likely to have high short interest.

"Short interest" is the quantity of shares that have been sold short by those who believe that the stock is going to go down.

To find a stock's short interest, go here and enter your ticker where it says "Get Key Statistics for," and then press "Go":

http://finance.yahoo.com/q/ks?s=VRX+Key+Statistics

Scroll down on the right side and you will see "Short % of float." This is the number of shares that have been sold short, divided by the float (which we defined above).

A widely hated stock will often have a short interest as percentage of float that is anywhere from 10% to 50% or even more.

Short sellers are usually pretty smart people. When a stock keeps hitting new 52 week lows and it has a high short interest, you want to stay away (or maybe go short yourself). Valeant (VRX) is a perfect example of this.

Short sellers are smart, but they are not infallible. When a stock with a high short interest starts hitting new highs, short sellers will be forced to buy back their shorts, whether they were right about the company or not.

And when they do, the stock will often explode higher. High short interest is simply more fuel for a rocket stock.

Many of the smartest people were short internet stocks in 1999 and early 2000. Although they were right about the stocks being overvalued, many were still forced to cover their shorts. It was this short covering that contributed to many of the explosive moves higher in early 2000.

To summarize:

- **Stocks that are widely hated, especially if they have high short interest, have the potential to move much higher.**
- **Don't avoid a rocket stock just because it makes you feel sick to your stomach, or because you have intellectual reasons why it is a bad investment.**
- **Doing the hardest thing frequently pays the best in the stock market.**

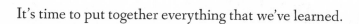

It's time to put together everything that we've learned.

The following conditions are absolutely required for a stock to have the potential to be a rocket stock:

- **The stock must be hitting new 52-week highs, or new all-time highs.**
- **There was a surge in daily volume (and maybe a daily gap) that confirmed the original break-out to new highs.**
- **The stock is trading above its 50-day moving average.**
- **The stock's 50-day moving average is above its 200-day moving average.**

The following conditions are extremely helpful, but not required:

- **The stock has a market cap of $4 billion or less.**

- The stock has a small float (where the float is 20% or less of the total shares outstanding).
- The stock and/or its industry are widely hated, especially by you.
- The stock has a short interest as a percentage of float that is greater than 10%.
- The SPY and/or QQQ is trading above its 50-day moving average.
- The SPY's and/or QQQ's 50-day moving average is above its 200-day moving average.

Let's consider another example. On March 11, 2016, ULTA gapped to new all-time highs on daily volume that was 4.75 times greater than its 60-day average daily volume:

You can also view an online version of this chart here:

https://www.tradingview.com/x/OMrcON9F/

On the day of the gap, ULTA closed above the 50-day moving average, and its 50-day moving average was trading above its 200-day moving average, so it was clearly in an uptrend as we define it.

On that day, ULTA closed at 191.62. Today, as I write this on June 9, 2016, ULTA is trading at 240.

You can see that once a stock gaps up on high volume, it is likely to do it again in the near future. ULTA did this on March 11, 2016 and then again on May 27, 2016.

Even if you did not participate in the first gap, there was plenty of time to get on board for the second gap.

When ULTA first gapped up, the SPY and QQQ were officially in downtrends. Over the last few months, as the SPY and QQQ have begun new uptrends, ULTA has become even stronger (hence, its second gap-up).

At this point, ULTA is definitely a market leader: it holds its ground when the market sells off, then gets even stronger when the market recovers.

Here's another amazing rocket stock. On March 15, 2016, CPXX gapped to a new all-time high on daily volume that was 35 times (!) greater than its 60-day average daily volume:

You can also view an online version of this chart here:

http://www.tradingview.com/x/JTcKB3sX/

On the day of the gap, CPXX closed at 8.94, which was above its 50-day moving average. Only the day before, CPXX had closed at 1.68. Talk about a difficult gap-up to buy!

On the day of its gap, the 50-day moving average was still trading below its 200-day moving average, so it was not yet time to buy the stock.

Four days later on March 18, the 50-day moving average finally crossed over the 200-day moving average, and the stock itself closed at 8.70, which was still above its 50-day moving average.

So the stock was in an uptrend, and it was time to buy at 8.70.

On top of that, CPXX had a market cap of just $316 million, which put it well below the suggested $4 billion market cap.

Today, as I write this on June 9, 2016, CPXX is trading at 30.15, after having received a buyout offer from Jazz Pharmaceuticals. That is up 246% from our entry in less than 3 months.

The smart money probably knew that a buyout was in the works, which is why they were comfortable driving the stock repeatedly to new all-time highs.

So what does CPXX actually do?

From Yahoo Finance:

"Celator Pharmaceuticals, Inc., a clinical stage biopharmaceutical company, develops therapies to treat cancer. Its proprietary drug ratio technology platform, CombiPlex, enables the rational design and rapid evaluation of optimized combinations incorporating traditional chemotherapies, as well as molecularly targeted agents to deliver enhanced anti-cancer activity. The company's product pipeline includes VYXEOS, a nano-scale liposomal formulation of irinotecan:floxuridine, which is in Phase III clinical testing for the treatment of acute myeloid leukemia; CPX-351, a liposomal formulation of cytarabine:daunorubicin, which is in Phase III study for the treatment of acute myeloid leukemia; and CPX-1, a liposomal formulation of irinotecan:floxuridine that has completed Phase II study for the treatment of colorectal cancer. Its preclinical stage product candidate is CPX-8, a hydrophobic docetaxel prodrug nanoparticle formulation for vitro and vivo studies."

If you did not understand that paragraph, you are not alone.

Fortunately, you did not need to have any technical knowledge about cancer therapy to participate in this rocket stock's rise.

You only needed to understand that when a stock gaps up to new all-time highs on high volume, something very important is usually about to happen.

Let's finish up with a very familiar rocket stock.

A few months before the financial crisis began, Apple peaked at

28.99 (split-adjusted) on December 27, 2007. It was not to see that level again until it closed at 29.27 on above-average volume on October 21, 2009.

On that day, Apple was trading above its 50-day moving average, and its 50-day moving average was above its 200-day moving average. It was clearly in a strong uptrend.

If you entered at the close at 29.27 and held on until the 50-day moving average crossed back below the 200-day moving average (on December 7, 2012 when Apple closed at 76.18), you made 160% on your money.

We'll discuss more about when to take profits in the next section.

Before we end, it is important to discuss position sizing, profit taking, and risk management.

Everyone is in a different financial situation, so be sure to consult with a financial advisor before trading.

And be sure to trade only with money that you can afford to lose, especially when you are just getting started with rocket stocks.

If you are a beginner, you might allocate 10% of your account to each trade. So if you have $10,000 in your account, you could put $1,000 into each new rocket stock that you find.

If you use a 10% stop loss on each of these positions, you will be risking 1% of your whole account ($100). That is a reasonable amount to risk on a trade for a beginner.

More advanced or aggressive traders will want to increase their position size when the stars align and the perfect rocket stock appears. Many fortunes were made by those who were able to bet big on Apple, Tesla, Netflix, and many other names.

As the great trader Stanley Druckenmiller says, "It takes courage to be a pig."

If you are really aggressive, you can buy at-the-money calls (or do a risk reversal) on a rocket stock. Shoot me an email if you need help learning how to do this: matt@trader.university.

Knowing when to take profits is always the most difficult part of trading rocket stocks. You will have to learn what makes you most comfortable, but here are some possible suggestions:

- Take profits when you are so excited and happy that you can't sleep.
- Take profits if a stock moves up 100% in 2 weeks or less.
- Take profits when you are up 300% on a trade.
- Take profits when your friends who hated the trade now begin to love the trade.

- Take profits when CNBC begins to praise the stock a bit too much.
- Take profits when a taxi driver or barber tells you to buy the stock.
- Exit (with a profit or loss) when the stock closes below its 50-day moving average. Use this method to capture shorter moves.
- Exit (with a profit or loss) when the stock closes below its 200-day moving average. Use this method to capture longer moves.
- Exit (with a profit or loss) when the 50-day moving average crosses below the 200-day moving average. Use this method to capture longer moves.
- Use a 10-day or 20-day exponential moving average as a trailing stop. Exit when the stock has a daily close below this exponential moving average. Use this to capture shorter moves.
- You can also scale out of a profitable position. Sell 1/4 of your position every Monday for 4 weeks in a row, or something similar.
- Just be sure to never add to a losing position. Pick a stop loss level when you enter the trade and stick to it. Only losers average losers. Rocket stocks go up fast, but they can also go down fast. Honor your stop loss.
- Don't ever get too greedy, or let money rule your life. Use the money that you make from rocket stocks to help other people.

Rocket stocks have been a phenomenal money-making machine for the past 20 years. I hope that you will enjoy trading them as much as I do.

If you have questions about a potential rocket stock, shoot me an email: matt@trader.university.

If you're looking at a rocket stock, there's a very good chance that I'm trading it.

Shoot me an email, and we can compare notes.

FOUR

DAY SNIPER TRADING (MY FAVORITE DAY TRADING STRATEGY)

Day trading is the fastest way to learn how the markets actually work.

If you love the markets, and are willing to follow them every day, you can learn to day trade profitably.

In the process, you will learn an enormous amount about the markets and about your own personal psychology.

The markets are the best tutor that I know.

And when you've put in your time, you will begin to make money.

On a good day, you will sit down at your trading desk at 9:45 am

EST, buy 3,000 shares of a stock, and watch it immediately pop 50 cents.

Ten minutes later, you will sell the stock and pocket $1,500.

It will be 9:55 am on a Monday morning, and you will already have made more money than the average American makes in a week.

Of course, if the trade goes against you, you will have lost more money than the average American makes in a week.

I want you to make money, instead of losing it.

So I am going to teach you a day trading strategy that will help to tilt the odds in your favor.

This strategy is called the "Day Sniper."

It is one of my "bread and butter trades" that I've relied on regularly to pay the bills over the years.

It is easy to learn, simple to follow, and it will teach you the discipline that is essential to becoming a successful full-time trader.

Once you master the basic strategy, you will learn to alter the strategy to make it fit your own particular style of trading.

The Day Sniper can be used in conjunction with candlestick formations, moving averages, Bollinger Bands, Parabolic SAR, and other indicators that I discuss in my trading courses.

But for now, it is most important to master the basic strategy.

Day trading can be an emotional roller-coaster. More than 90% of day traders lose money over time.

I want you to be part of the 10% that makes money.

And so I am going to give you everything that you need to get started.

First, learn the basic strategy.

Then practice in a paper trading account, or with very small amounts of money.

As you begin to make money, gradually increase the amount of money that you are trading with.

And only then begin to experiment by adding variations to the basic strategy.

Maybe you will delay your initial entry, to try to get a more favorable price.

Maybe you will add to a position on an intraday counter-trend move in order to increase your profits.

Or maybe you will cover your short in the middle of the day, after an especially violent move down, in order to avoid an end-of-day short-covering rally that might eat into your profits.

The more you practice, the more you will be able to bend the rules and trust your gut.

But for now, it's time to learn the basic strategy.

The Day Sniper day trading strategy takes advantage of a basic fact of market structure:

It takes time for big players to enter and exit their positions.

If a mutual fund is holding millions of shares of the stock XYZ, it cannot simply press a button to exit its position.

If XYZ has just reported some very bad news in their latest earnings report, the mutual fund is in a tough spot.

It will take hours, days, or maybe even weeks for the mutual fund to exit its position, depending on the liquidity of the stock.

And the same holds true for a stock that has just reported very good news in its latest earnings report.

If a large mutual fund wants to open a new position (or increase its existing position) in this stock, it will take hours, days, or maybe even weeks for it to do so.

The good news is that smaller traders like you and I can take advantage of these slow, lumbering giants.

Hence, the Day Sniper strategy.

Let's start with an example.

On November 10, 2016, NVIDIA (NVDA) reported much better than expected earnings.

The CEO Jen-Hsun Huang said in the conference call:

"We had a breakout quarter—record revenue, record margins, and record earnings were driven by strength across all product lines."

Right before earnings were released, NVDA had closed at 67.77. After the bullish earnings announcement, the stock immediately traded up about 10% in the after-market trading session.

The next morning, the stock opened up even higher-- at 79.51, up more than 17% from the closing price of the day before.

At this point, even though the stock had already moved up sharply, there were still many institutional investors (mutual funds, hedge funds, and pension funds) who wanted to own more NVDA.

There were many different reasons for this.

Some wanted to be able to show their investors that they owned a lot of a currently fashionable stock.

Some had been short the stock, betting on a bearish earnings report, and now needed to buy shares to cover their shorts.

Some may not have owned any shares, or owned too few shares, and now wanted to increase their positions, because they believed that the company's cash flow or return on assets had fundamentally changed for the better.

Whatever the reason, many institutional investors now needed to buy a lot of NVDA shares.

The problem?

Well, these institutional investors needed to buy millions of shares, which were simply not available all at once.

As a result, they would all need to nibble on the stock, buying a little at a time.

This is where smaller traders like you and I have such a great advantage.

We can run ahead of these slow, lumbering giants, scoop up some shares for ourselves, and then later sell them back to the institutional investors—at a higher price.

This is how the Day Sniper strategy works:

1. Find a stock that is gapping up on good news (like a bullish earnings report).

2. Wait until 15 minutes after the market's open, and note the stock's price at that time.
3. Put in a limit order to buy the stock at that price.
4. If you are not filled in the next 15 minutes, cancel your order and walk away.
5. If you are filled, hold on to the stock and then take profits one minute before the market closes at the end of the day (profit target).
6. Exit the stock early if it trades below the low price of that first 15 minutes of morning trading (stop loss).

It's that simple.

The strategy takes advantage of a stock's tendency to keep moving in the same direction of its morning gap.

What is a gap?

It is simply when a stock moves up or down sharply, leaving a "gap" in the chart that separates it from its previous trading range.

This is what a gap looks like:

You can see from this chart that NVDA had never traded above 72.50 before.

All of a sudden after the bullish earnings report, it was trading in the high 70's. You can see the striking look of the gap in the chart above.

To trade this strategy, I like to use a chart with 15-minute candlesticks.

You can set up a chart like this using a free service like www.freestockcharts.com.

If you need help setting up your chart, check out my Free Trading Tutorial.

I like to include at least the last 20 days of trading on my 15-minute candlestick chart for the following reason:

You should only take the trade if the stock gaps up above the highest high of the last 20 trading days (or gaps below the lowest low of the last 20 trading days, as we will see in a later section on shorting stocks).

A gap that is this dramatic will only occur when there is excessive demand for the stock by buyers.

It will often take the entire day for this excessive demand to be met. This will cause the stock to continue to drift higher, as institutional investors continue to buy the stock.

Let's return to our 15-minute candlestick chart.

You will want to enter your limit order to buy the stock at the closing price of that first 15-minute candlestick.

Your stop loss will be the low of that first 15-minute candlestick. If at any point during the day the stock trades below this price, you should sell it immediately.

If you are not stopped out, you should hold on to the stock until the end of the day. Sell the stock about one or two minutes before the market closes.

If you choose to hold the stock overnight, you're no longer a day trader.

You've become a swing trader.

And that's another strategy for another book.

When you are first starting out, learn the discipline of always exiting at the end of the day.

Go completely to cash, whether the trade has made or lost money, and you will sleep better at night.

Now let's return to the details of our NVDA trade.

After reporting good earnings, the stock gaps up the next morning:

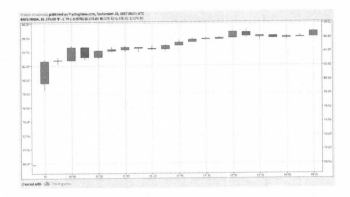

The candlestick on the left shows the first 15 minutes of trading. It opens at 79.51, trades as low as 78.50, as high as 82.82, and then closes at 82.60.

As you can see, when a stock first opens in the morning (6:30 am PST or 9:30 am EST), there is usually a lot of chaos and volatility.

That's why I like to wait until 6:45 am PST (or 9:45 am EST), when the market has been open for 15 minutes, to place my first trade.

So at 6:45 am, we place a limit order to buy NVDA at 82.60 (the closing price of that first 15-minute candlestick).

Within the next 15 minutes, we are filled on our order. We set a mental stop loss at 78.50 (the low of that first 15-minute candlestick). If the stock trades below that price during the day, we are out.

We now hold on to NVDA for the rest of the day, and sell it 1 minute before the market closes at approximately 87.72.

We have captured 5.12 points (87.72-82.60), which comes out to $512 if we've traded 100 shares.

After commissions, that's about $500 net profit for the day.

You would have needed approximately $8,265 in your trading account to buy 100 shares of NVDA at 82.60 (82.60 times 100 plus $5 commission to enter).

There are about 252 trading days in a year, so if we can do this every day, we will be making $126,000 per year.

Even if we can do only half as well (since there will be days when we lose money), we'll still be making $63,000 per year.

To put that in perspective, the median household in the US makes roughly $52,000 per year.

You may wish to trade less aggressively than this when you are first getting started.

So for example, if your targeted entry price is 82.60 and your stop is at 78.50, you will be risking 4.10 points on the trade.

When you are first getting started, it is wise not to risk more than 1% of your trading account on each trade.

So if you are trading a $10,000 account, don't risk more than 1%, which is $100.

If you are risking 4.10 points on this NVDA trade, you should only buy ($100/4.10) or about 24 shares of stock on this trade.

If you buy 24 shares of NVDA at 82.60 and get stopped out at 78.50, you will have lost 4.10 points on 24 shares or about $98 (4.10 times 24).

The closer your entry price is to your stop loss, the more shares you will be able to buy.

For this reason, many traders will only take this trade if they think they can make at least twice the amount that they are risking.

Now let's turn to another example of the Day Sniper strategy at work.

Before the market opened on Tuesday, April 25, 2017, McDonald's (MCD) reported earnings and revenues that beat expectations. All-day breakfast and new sizes for the Big Mac helped to drive up comparable store sales.

So how do we know when a company's earnings report actually beats the expectations?

We can read about the actual EPS reported, and compare it to the analyst consensus projections.

But the only way to be certain that a company has actually beaten the expectations is to witness its stock gapping up in the first 15 minutes of trading like MCD did:

The first 15-minute candlestick of the day closed at 138.87, and had a low of 137.18.

And so fifteen minutes into the trading day, we enter a limit order to buy 100 shares of MCD at 138.87. We are filled on our order immediately.

We then make a mental note that our stop loss is at 137.18 (the low of that first 15-minute candlestick). If MCD trades below that, we will exit our position immediately.

MCD continues to grind higher for most of the day. We exit our position right before the market closes at 141.70.

On this trade, we've captured 2.83 points (141.70-138.87), which is $283 (on 100 shares) before commissions.

It shouldn't cost you more than $5 to enter the trade, and $5 to exit the trade if you are using a good online broker like TradeKing or Interactive Brokers. That leaves you with $273 in profits for the day, after commissions.

Although I haven't used it myself, I've also heard good things about the Robinhood app which allows you to trade for free—no commissions!

One of the nice things about the Day Sniper strategy is that it can also be used to trade stocks that are gapping down.

This works especially well in a bear market, when all stocks have a tendency to trade down.

If you learn to trade from both the long and short sides, it will ensure that you will be able to make money in both bull and bear markets.

Let's look at an example of how to short a stock using the strategy.

On March 21, 2017 Nike (NKE) closed at 58.01. It then reported lower than expected quarterly revenue numbers in its earnings report.

The next morning, the stock gapped down 5.60%, opening at 54.76:

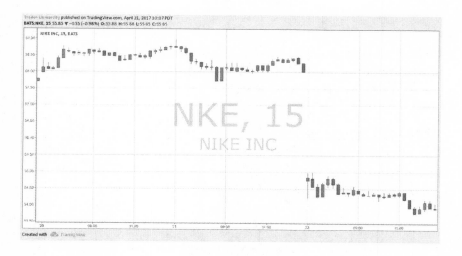

In this case, an investor's pain is our gain. I am going to show you how to profit from the stock continuing to sell off for the rest of the day.

The first 15-minute candlestick opened at 54.76, closed at 54.85, and traded as high as 55.00 and as low as 54.23.

In this case, we will be shorting the stock. We will use the order type "sell short" using a limit order at 54.85.

When we are filled, we will place a mental stop loss at the high of that first 15-minute candlestick at 55.00. If the stock trades above that level during the day, we will exit our position immediately.

To exit a short position, we will want to use the order type "buy to cover."

If we are not stopped out, we will wait to exit the position until about 1 minute before the market closes.

In this case, we shorted NKE at 54.85 and covered our short at 53.93 just before the market closed. Trading 100 shares, we captured 0.92 points, or about $92.00 before commissions.

Many new traders are confused about what it means to short a stock.

It's actually quite simple.

When we are buying a stock, we want to buy low and sell high. That's how the money is made.

When we are shorting a stock, we simply reverse the steps:

We first sell high, and then try to buy low.

So how do we sell something that we don't already own?

To short a stock, it is first necessary for the stock to be available to borrow from your broker.

If you have opened up a "margin account" with your broker, you will be able to short sell stocks in your account.

The process of borrowing the shares is usually seamless. There is often a list that you can check to see if the shares are available for shorting.

If it is a well-known name, it should not be a problem to get the shares.

If it is a lesser known name, it may be more difficult.

Be sure to check if there are special fees associated with borrowing a stock to short (such as stock loan fees). Call your brokerage to find out.

Let's look at another example of short selling.

Early on April 18, 2017, Goldman Sachs reported a rare earnings miss. In fact, both earnings and revenues came in below expectations.

The previous day, the stock had closed at 226.26. After reporting earnings before the market opened on April 18, the stock gapped down over 3%, opening up at 219.32.

That open was its lowest trading level for more than the past 20 days:

The stock continued to drift lower for much of the rest of the day:

The opening 15-minute candlestick closed at 219.33 and had a high of 219.89.

This proved to be the perfect short trade, since the stop loss (219.89) was so close to the desired entry price (219.33).

So at 6:45 am, we entered an order to sell short 100 shares of GS at 219.33, and were filled.

The next 15-minute bar came close to stopping us out of the trade. It traded as high as 219.85, but fortunately did not breach the 219.89 level where we had (mentally) set our stop loss.

Before we go on, I should remind you to never actually enter your stop loss order directly into the market. If you do this, you run the risk of someone seeing your stop order and trying to run the market to take out your stop.

Rather, write down your stop loss level on a piece of paper, and keep it next to your computer.

If the stock hits that level, exit your position using a limit order that is placed just a penny or two above where the market is currently trading (if you are buying to cover).

If you're desperate to get out, you can also enter a market order, but that is more risky. A market order will get you out, but sometimes at a price that is much further away from the current stock price than you would like.

To get back to our GS trade: we got short at 219.33, and fortunately did not get stopped out when the stock traded as high as 219.85.

The stock continued to move lower until it hit an all-day low of 213.18 at 10:05 am PST.

I have found that around 10 am PST (1 pm EST) can be a great time to take profits, on both the long and short side. You will often end up exiting your trade at the low (or high) of the day.

I am not sure why this anomaly exists, but it may have something to do with traders taking a break for lunch around 12 pm to 1 pm EST. When there is lower liquidity, it is easier for the market to trade more irrationally.

That being said, if you held on to the GS trade until just before the market closed, you still ended up doing very well. You were able to cover your short at 215.59, capturing 3.74 points, or about $374 on 100 shares before commissions.

If you exited at 10 am, you made more like 5.50 points, or $550.

Now that you understand the basic Day Sniper strategy, you probably want to know where you can find the best stocks to trade using this strategy.

Well, for the Day Sniper strategy, we are looking for stocks that have just reported earnings, or some other significant news.

My favorite place to find possible candidates for the strategy is the "Trending" list at the top of StockTwits.com (you will need to open a free account with them to view it):

Next to the word "Trending," you can see a list of tickers. If you look here after 1 or 2 pm PST, you are sure to find some stocks that have just reported earnings (assuming that it is earnings season), or that are on the move due to significant news.

You can click on each ticker to see how much the stock is trading up or down. If it is trading more than 3% up or down, search for the ticker on Google News to see what news is moving the stock. You may also see the news in the StockTwits stream itself.

Perhaps it is an earning beat or miss, or perhaps something significant has happened at the company, like the CEO or CFO leaving.

Or perhaps they have "pre-announced" that earnings will come in higher or lower than previously expected.

You can use this to start making a list of stocks that you will want to watch the next morning during the first 15 minutes of trading.

You may be tempted to buy some of these stocks in the after-market hours of trading.

When you are just starting out, you should resist this temptation.

Often a stock will trade significantly higher in the after-hours market after reporting earnings, and then crash 30 minutes later during the earnings call if negative forward guidance is being given.

The after-hours market is extremely volatile, and anything can happen.

Sometimes there may be little or no liquidity (i.e. it will be next to impossible to buy or sell the stock at the price that you are seeing).

It is much better to wait until the following morning, and to watch how the stock trades during that first 15-minute candlestick.

When you are more advanced, and have the courage of your convictions, you may choose to trade in the after-market or pre-market— especially if you follow the company closely, have listened to the earnings call, and are extremely familiar with the company's financial statements, as well as with the industry as a whole.

Until then, stick to the basic Day Sniper strategy.

Another great place to find potential candidates for this strategy is to look at this screener when the market first opens in the morning:

http://www.finviz.com/screener.ashx?
v=111&f=ta_perf_d5u&ft=3&o=-price

This screener will provide you with a list of stocks that are trading up more than 5% on the day. You can also change the settings to include stocks that are moving up 10% or more, or down 5% or more.

Once you find a stock that looks interesting, it is important to check the chart to make sure that it is gapping above the last 20-day high, or below the last 20-day low.

At the same time, you can watch the first 15-minute candlestick form, and get ready to place your order at 6:45 am PST if the stock meets all of the necessary criteria.

You can also find good candidates by keeping track of the earnings calendar of stocks. Here are some great places to check:

http://finance.yahoo.com/calendar/earnings

http://www.morningstar.com/earnings/earnings-calendar.aspx

http://www.nasdaq.com/earnings/earnings-calendar.aspx

http://www.marketwatch.com/news/markets/earningswatch.asp

This site will even send you an email alert when a particular ticker reports significant news or earnings:

https://seekingalpha.com/earnings/earnings-calendar

And this site is especially good for finding earnings surprises among well-known names:

http://www.cnbc.com/earnings-surprises/

Most companies will report earnings after the market closes. If you go over these websites every evening, you can create a short list of stocks that you will want to be watching when the market opens the next day.

Some stocks will report earnings in the morning before the stock market opens. These names will also show up in the earnings calendar, and on StockTwits if there is significant movement and interest in the stock.

It is now time to examine a challenge that you may encounter if you are a trader in the U.S. with a small account size.

If you are a trader in the U.S., and you make 4 or more round-trip day trades within a 5-day period in a margin account, you will end up being labeled by the authorities as a "pattern day trader."

A pattern day trader is required by law to maintain a balance of at least $25,000 in his account at all times.

New traders are often discouraged by this rule, which seems to set up a classic catch-22: how can I ever get to $25,000 in my trading account, if you won't let me day trade with a lesser amount?

Fortunately, there are a few ways around this rule.

Before I tell you these ways, I should emphasize that I am not providing legal advice, or advising you in any way what you should actually do with your own trading account. That is a matter between you, your broker, and your financial advisor, of course.

But what I can do here is to tell you what has worked for people that I know.

I know of 5 methods that may be used to bypass the pattern day trader rule.

Method #1

Do your day trading in a "cash account," rather than a "margin account."

In this scenario, you will unfortunately have to wait 3 days after you exit a trade for the cash to be back in your account in order to do another trade. You will also not be able to employ any margin (leverage) in your account. For these reasons, this is probably not the best method.

Method #2

Do only 3 day trades within a rolling 5 business day period.

So if for example you did one day trade on Monday, one on Tuesday, and one on Wednesday, you should not do another day trade until the following Monday (i.e. 3 day trades over 5 trading days).

You can still make a lot of money this way, and start to build up your account. I like this method the most because you can still use leverage (up to 2x in a margin account), but you are forced to trade less frequently and to be more discriminating, taking only the best trades.

Be very careful: if you do a 4th trade within this same rolling 5-day period, your account will be flagged as a pattern day trader account. You will then receive a margin call from your broker that requires you to bring your account balance up to $25,000 within 5 business days.

If you fail to meet this margin call, different things could happen depending on your broker. In most cases, your buying power will be restricted for 90 days, or until the margin call is met (the account balance is brought up to $25,000).

You should call your own broker to find out exactly how they handle the pattern day trader rule.

You can read about how TradeKing handles the pattern day trader rule here:

http://www.tradeking.com/investing/day-trading-rules

Method #3

Hold your trades overnight, especially if you have already done 3 day trades in the last rolling 5-day period.

If you hold a trade overnight, it will not count towards the 4 trades, since an overnight trade is not a day trade.

Unfortunately, holding a stock overnight will definitely expose you to more risk. You may make more money as a result, but you can also lose money.

Literally anything can happen overnight in the worlds of geopolitics or business.

On the other hand, if you are using a trailing stop in your trade, and you have still not been stopped out by the end of the day, you may wish to hold overnight.

Or if the stock is finishing at the highs (or lows, if you are short the stock) of the day, you may also wish to hold the position overnight. These strong moves will often continue overnight and into the opening minutes of the next trading day.

Method #4

Split your cash between two separate brokerage accounts.

So if you have $10,000, you could open up an account at TradeKing with $5,000 and an account at Interactive Brokers with $5,000.

Using this method, you can do 6 day trades in a rolling 5 business day period (3 trades in each account as in method #3).

Method #5

This final method will allow you to do an unlimited number of day trades.

First, split your trading account across 2 brokerages as in method #5. Put $5,000 at TradeKing or wherever, and $5,000 at Interactive Brokers, or wherever.

But in this case, you will do something especially sneaky. Let's say that today you bought 100 shares of NVDA in your TradeKing account. At the end of the day, instead of selling the shares, simply sell short 100 shares of NVDA in your Interactive Brokers account.

This will zero-out your exposure to the stock, in effect taking profits. If NVDA falls overnight, you will lose money in your TradeKing account, but you will make back the same amount of money on your short NVDA position in your Interactive Brokers account.

The following morning, you can exit your long NVDA position and your short NVDA position. Since each one was held overnight, neither trade will count toward your 3 allowed day trades.

This latter method may just be a bit too clever. I'll leave it up to your own judgment.

When you are first starting out, it might be better to stick to making 3 day trades over every rolling 5 trading day period.

Keep following the Day Sniper trading rules until you have learned to always stick to your stop loss.

And make sure that you exit your day trade every single time by the end of the trading day.

Remember that only losers hold a losing day trade overnight.

Once you have established this sort of trading discipline, feel free to experiment with different kinds of trailing stops like moving averages, Parabolic SAR, and 3-line break.

If you'd like to learn more about these advanced methods, you can also check out my course "Learn to Trade Stocks like a Pro" at http://www.trader.university.

FIVE
FROM SMALL BEGINNINGS TO GREAT WEALTH

We've covered a lot of ground in this book. I hope that you are ready to take this information and use it to start making money for yourself trading.

The best way to learn about trading is to just start doing it. Start with very small positions, and then slowly increase them as your capital (and your confidence!) increases.

There's no better way to learn than simply by doing.

And I'm here to help you on your journey to becoming a professional trader.

If you have questions, or just want to say hi, write to me at matt@trader.university

I love to hear from my readers, and I answer every email personally.

Before you go, I'd like to say "thank you" for purchasing this book and reading it all the way to the end.

If you enjoyed this book and found it useful, I'd be very grateful if you'd post an honest review on Amazon.

All that you need to do is to do is this:

- Go to **www.trader.university**
- Click on "Books."
- Click on "The Big Book of Stock Trading Strategies."
- Click on the blue link next to the yellow stars that says "customer reviews."
- You'll then see a gray button that says "Write a customer review."
- Click on that and you will be able to write your review and submit it to Amazon.

Thank you so much for writing a review of my book on Amazon.

Your Amazon review will help other readers like yourself to find my books.

If you would like to learn more ways to make money in the markets, check out my other Kindle books on the next page.

KEEP LEARNING WITH THESE TRADING BOOKS

The Little Black Book of Stock Market Secrets

Invest Like Warren Buffett: Powerful Strategies for Building Wealth

Monthly Cash Machine: Powerful Strategies for Selling Options in Bull and Bear Markets

Covered Calls Made Easy: Generate Monthly Cash Flow by Selling Options

To purchase these books and more, simply go to www.trader.university and click on "Books."

YOUR FREE GIFT

Thanks for purchasing my book!

As a way of showing my appreciation, I want to send you a FREE BONUS CHAPTER that contains everything that you need to start using my stock trading strategies.

In this free bonus chapter, you will learn:

- How to use online screeners to find the best stocks to trade
- How to set up a trading chart using free online resources
- Tricks to make the trading strategies even more profitable
- A free video tutorial on the Day Sniper day trading strategy
- And much, much more

Enter your email at the link below and I will send you a free copy of this Bonus Chapter:

http://www.trader.university/big-book/

ABOUT THE AUTHOR

Hi there!

My name is Matthew Kratter.

I am the founder of Trader University, and the best-selling author of multiple books on trading and investing.

I have more than 20 years of trading experience, including working at multiple hedge funds.

Most individual traders and investors are at a huge disadvantage when it comes to the markets. Most are unable to invest in hedge funds. Yet, when they trade their own money, they are competing against computer algorithms, math PhD's, and multi-billion dollar hedge funds.

I've been on the inside of many hedge funds. I know how professional traders and investors think and approach the markets. And I am committed to sharing their trading strategies with you in my books and courses.

When I am not trading or writing new books, I enjoy skiing, hiking, and otherwise hanging out in the Rocky Mountains with my wife, kids, and dogs.

If you enjoyed this book, you may also enjoy my other Kindle titles, which are available here:

www.trader.university

Or send me an email at matt@trader.university.

I would love to hear from you.

DISCLAIMER

While the author has used his best efforts in preparing this book, he makes no representations or warranties with respect to the accuracy or completeness of the contents of this book and specifically disclaims any implied warranties or merchantability or fitness for a particular purpose. The advice and strategies contained herein may not be suitable for your situation. You should consult with a legal, financial, tax, or other professional where appropriate. Neither the publisher nor the author shall be liable for any loss of profit or any other commercial damages, including but not limited to special, incidental, consequential, or other damages.

This book is for educational purposes only. The views expressed are those of the author alone, and should not be taken as expert instruction or commands. The reader is responsible for his or her own actions.

Adherence to all applicable laws and regulations, including

international, federal, state, and local laws governing professional licensing, business practices, advertising, and all other aspects of doing business in the US, Canada, or any other jurisdiction is the sole responsibility of the purchaser or reader.

Neither the author nor the publisher assumes any responsibility or liability whatsoever on the behalf of the purchaser or reader of these materials.

Any perceived slight of any individual or organization is purely unintentional.

Trading and day trading can be extremely risky.

Trading and day trading are generally not appropriate for someone of limited resources and limited investment or trading experience and low risk tolerance.

You should be prepared to lose all of the funds that you use for trading or day trading. In particular, you should not fund your trading or day-trading activities with retirement savings, student loans, second mortgages, emergency funds, funds set aside for purposes such as education or home ownership, or funds required to meet your living expenses.

Past performance is not necessarily indicative of future performance. Forex, futures, stock, and options trading is not appropriate for everyone. There is a substantial risk of loss associated with trading these markets. Losses can and will occur. No system or methodology has ever been developed that can guarantee profits or ensure freedom from losses. Nor will it likely ever be. No representation or implication is being made that using the methodologies or systems or the information contained within this book will generate profits or ensure freedom from losses. The information contained in this book is for educational purposes only and should NOT be taken as investment advice. Examples presented here are not solicitations to buy or sell. The author, publisher, and all affiliates assume no responsibility for your trading results.

There is a high risk in trading.

71912571R00067

Made in the USA
Lexington, KY
26 November 2017